AF479219

Entries

Raymond Oliver

ENTRIES

DAVID R. GODINE · BOSTON
A Godine Poetry Chapbook
Fourth Series

First published in 1982 by
DAVID R. GODINE, PUBLISHER, INC.
306 Dartmouth Street
Boston, Massachusetts 02116

Library of Congress Cataloging in Publication Data

Oliver, Raymond, 1936-
    Entries.
    (A Godine poetry chapbook; 4th ser.)
    I. Title.
PS3565.L516E5   811'.54   80-83948
ISBN 0-87923-366-4

Some of these poems first appeared in the following pub-
lications: *Arizona Quarterly, The Berkeley Poetry Review, Canto,
The Compass, The Dalhousie Review, Denver Quarterly, The
Greensboro Review, Iowa Review, Mississippi Review, Occident,
Prairie Schooner, Sequoia, The Southern Review,* and *The
Threepenny Review.*

Printed in the United States of America

Contents

For Mary Anne, Once Again

Discourse on Method

Not to write poems, but to state,
Like truth, the figures of my thought,
The icons that illuminate
My book of hours; to define,
With candid artifice, each line,
Each tangent, till what I have wrought
Stands clear; to fix in words my essence,
Which is the gist of all I know,
Against the subtle deliquescence
Of time—I have no more to show.
These are the motives of my soul,
The parts, to which conforms the whole.

Procedures

1. AGGRESSION

I grasp for words, knit them to verse,
And with this close-wrought net I stalk
        the Muse—
Only to see my game disperse
Between the lines, free, and for none to use.

2. PLAYING MOZART

To put one's fingers firmly on his soul,
To get by hand the movements of his thought—
Contours and peaks that only he could plot—
Is to be played by him; to lose control.

3

Though made of wood, this pencil
Is quicker than the fingers
Of fire, and more prehensile:
With it, I probe what lingers
Of my experience,
And grasp its fleeting sense.

Portuguese

This is no tongue to turn a compliment,
Or twist a curse too graceful to resent,
Or speak in flames grandly of heaven and hell;
Its sound is intimate, like the frying-smell
Of garlic. With liquids like a heavy wine,
It speaks of sweet-loaves, olives packed in brine,
Chestnuts and squash; its consonants
    are blurred,
Nasals insinuating, diphthongs slurred
With overtones, like some ignoble wish;
It is a language of linguiça, fish,
Mary, and Christ—staples on which to fatten
Both flesh and soul. Among the sons of Latin
It seems a country cousin, rich but crude;
Yet one must praise a tongue that savors food
And God with gusto: familial Portuguese,
In whose irregular moods I feel at ease.

On Reading Sixteenth-Century Verse

After a while, sweetness begins to pall;
I seek plain herbs amid Petrarcan bowers.
For epigrams are weeds among the flowers,
Intruders in the garden since the Fall
Whose only pretense is medicinal.

Footnote

Goethe and Hölderlin
Express more than they mean.

The Mayor of Casterbridge

I read it one November long ago
In muted, stripped New England, in a cracked
And acrid hard-bound book. It didn't snow
But should have; that was all my reading lacked.

What stays is Henchard's frumenty, his grain,
His wagons; dark-eaved cobbled Autumn streets
Muffled in frost or 'during wind and rain';
A mood of shingle when the tide retreats,

But hearty. It's not the Tragic Theme that stays;
Only this texture of the book, those days.

Gone is the tact
Of former time.
Not 'strong' but slack,
The poet's line
No longer holds
Experience,
Which—subtle, old,
Of power immense—
Now bends his forms
At its own pleasure.
We have no norm;
The pulse that measures
Civilization
Is wild, erratic—
As a heart-patient
Might seem ecstatic.

The Focus

So have I kept myself in mind,
Moment by moment, that I know
These changing selves not as a line
That graphs my progress young to old,
But as a focussing on and for
The world. It burns extremely here,
When I am mindful of my chore—
A consummation that appears
The less consumed as used and needed,
Like books that live through endless reading.

South

Travelling in the West, one crosses space.
One sky extends from Kansas to the coast;
Under it, variations not of place
But of the earth. Towns are alike; at most,
Their sizes vary. What one sees is land,
A work of mountains, plains, rock, snow,
        and sand.

Travelling South one enters a preserve,
A place where history is, an alien state
With misty depths and switchbacks to unnerve
Outsiders; not to cross, but penetrate.
One notes details, in which not anywhere
But South inheres: how smoke hangs in the air,

How much persists—old squares with
        courthouse, men
All day on benches, twilight, custom, heat. . . .
It's like a childhood book one reads again,
Heavy with mystery, glory, and defeat;
Imagination's place, where memories run
Like colors in the downward evening sun.

The Expedition to Mobile Bay, 1558–61

Tristan de Luna, Tristan of the Moon,
It seems, now, an affair of words: Velasco,
Your pattern, patron, and boss, evokes fiasco,
And you some starry fantasy of doom.
Bells and incense waft you from Veracruz,
Bedizened masts like swaying Christmas-trees,
With banners, crosses, horses, cavalry,
A thousand settlers—all the more to lose.
You heave a hundred horses overboard
Even before the August hurricane
That pops your hulls and ropes like an insane
Beethoven on the strings and drums. It's scored
For dissonance and groans, your enterprise.
Who would believe that storm—you didn't, it
Was 'devil-work'—which blew your sodden ship,
Untouched, a gunshot inland? God relies
At times on madmen for his goodly schemes.
The faithful must have thought this for a while,
Tristan, as they, obedient, hammered piles
Into the muck, while insects from a dream
Of Bosch drove barbs into their melting flesh.
The hecatombs of food, tools, horses—these
Had been exacted by the mindless seas;
But now, his fabric cracking with the stress,
A man is sacrificing men, to the land
Or maybe to the moon. Poor Tristan, rapt
With America; your ropes and spars have snapped.
Your victims force you home, they will
     not understand.

Metamorphoses

for Eugene Walter, in memory of Mobile

1. SINISTER

Wragg Swamp, that once on blackest
    summer nights
Stood out with even blacker limbs intact
Though tattered, brooding on primeval life,
Raucous with cries, is now a housing-tract.

2. OLD CREOLE COTTAGE

It passed from everyday to picturesque
As ladies pass from youth to gentle eld—
So gracefully had walls and floorboards swelled,
Had tendrils laced with flowery arabesque
The doors and windows. Thus the loving tourist,
Aided by time, converts the commonplace
To art, pleasing all but the surly purist,
Who won't see bulge as curve or vines as lace.

3. A NOTE TO EUGENE, ON CITY PLANNERS ETC.

Mobile is turning into Anywhere;
We mourn it, with the squirrels of
    Bienville Square.
Planners, like virus born of some black humor,
Convert the city to a neon tumor,
Changing its shapely structure cell by cell
To shopping-center, parking-lot, motel.
So we move out, reactionaries both.
Only a change of place will check this growth.

St. Martinville

The edge of town is already stale; the square,
Fresh with decay like well-aged camembert,
Is so passé as almost to rescind
Our times, more truly than in *Gone With The Wind,*
Making Louisiana France again:
Façades without pretensions, broad and plain;
Arcades of wooden porches; church with saint.
The French is like the local aura—quaint,
Americanized around the edges, soft,
Gracefully worn.
                These qualities that waft
Like spirits of the region through the air:
I must extract their scents, while they are there.

House on Fowl River

Fowl River, brown and slow, does not reflect
But takes much in from trees bending above;
It changes leaf and seed, as they collect,
To fertile mud, in a long act of love.

Mute as its trees, the house exfoliates
Into a stream. It must dissolve in time,
But richly—changing past and passing states
To dream-stuff, in a mortal pantomime.

On Dauphin Island

For miles along the lucid beach
The Gulf of Mexico unrolls,
Piecemeal, in thin, illumined scrolls
Of surf, conveying ancient speech,

The message of the sea to land.
Its rhythm, colors, form are clear
And it repeats. I overhear,
With love, and need not understand.

At the Creek

to M.A., for K. and N.

Our childhood of the forties waits,
Just as we left it, at the creek.
We spread the cloth; daddy inflates
The inner-tube, which has a leak;
Run down the hot, unpainted pier—
Slivers, and cracks to crack our toes—
Now leap, leaving not toes but fear
Behind—splash/water up the nose;
Its coldness warms, at last feels dry,
Enclosing us like blurred brown air
(To swim within it is to fly,
Clumsily tumbling anywhere);
Then waterlogged ennui; then out.
Baloney, watermelon, cokes,
Hotdogs festooned with sauerkraut,
All relished like the games and jokes
With which our heads, like bellies, fill.
The pier we're playing on is steady;
It is a stage, but lasting still,
The plot and roles unaltered, ready.
No change; though others show us how
We were, and I am daddy now.

To My Family

I will not let your hours pass through mine
Like quick lunches with no distracting flavor.
You are my daily dinner served with wine;
Vital distraction, which I choose to savor.

To My Grandmother

Past ninety now, it is the night you dread,
Each night; you do not dare lie down in bed.
With your congested heart ready to break,
You sit upright, trying to stay awake
In hope of dawn. Take courage: you are right.
To live indeed, fix your eyes on the light.

After Long Separation

As distance separates,
So does experience,
Which nothing compensates.
Though friendship was intense,

Our absent-mindedness
Brings us to this strange state:
Bonds we have still, but less
Than those who live in hate

Yet live together. Age,
Novel as morning's frost,
Is on your face; I gauge
In you the life we've lost.

Words for António Raimundo de Oliveira

Your name, like Baudelaire's grand albatross,
Could not survive out of its element;
And part of you did not survive its loss.

The change to 'Tony Oliver' had rent
Your past from present, half from half,
    with shocks
That, shifting your articulation, bent

Both tongue and back. From warm volcanic rocks
Lush in the North Atlantic, you had come:
St. Michael, Azores—Islands of the Hawks.

Did the defending angel hover, dumb,
As you heaved barrels on the Boston docks?

To M.A.

You are my own iconoclast.
When I, poetic solipsist,
Would make you over, you resist;
My faithless images you cast
Back in my face, till I can see
That you are there, amending me.

Marriage

The harmony we serve,
In serving one another,
Wholly resounds within.
I am your practised lover,
Rubbing nerve on nerve
Like bow on violin.

Adam to Eve

Your strength and beauty flare out at your hips,
Which stretch your contoured belly wide, convex
Yet firm. I know your breasts, your eyes,
    your lips;
But these are not the substance of your sex.

Making my hand a compass, I can trace
A semicircle from your navel down:
Here is your womanhood, the holy place,
Whose central triangle of solid brown

Shockingly swells above surrounding skin,
More prominent than hips, and purposive;
For here you take, to cherish deep within,
The touch of life that I, your husband, give.

Jeremiad for St. Jerome

If you're in heaven, purified
Of all of you that should have died,
One wonders how much could be left.
By choice or temperament bereft
Of love, sex, friendship, honesty,
And courage, you slandered Melanie,
Jovinian—all who disagreed;
Betrayed Rufinus; out of need
To butter up the bishop, twisted
The words of Origen; resisted
The truth with lies and self-denial;
Detested women, all the while
Pressing virginity on girls
And rich widows. Those strings of pearls
You cast before us married swine:
Eat them and choke, line by pure line.

Newspaper Story

S.F. Chronicle, May 1973

A gifted San Francisco whore
Who, like a multipurpose fixture,
Can screw on table, bed, or floor
And be adjusted for the ease
Of six men on a high trapeze,
Is suffering from a nasty stricture:
The ad-men are no longer sure
Her face should advertise their soap,
Which is by figures, facts, and hope
Nearly synonymous with *pure.*
Such girls keep clean—if not her face,
Why don't they try some other place?

French Quarter, New Orleans

This stripper, now laid bare,
Makes with the Prince of Air
The two-backed beast,
Showing, with twist and jerk,
The god at work.
Her lover is not there;
But each believer, awed
And self-released,
Himself puts on the god.

Paradoxes

I am your mistress Circe,
Whom your desires possess.
I have you at my mercy;
But I am merciless.

Across from the De Young Museum

Golden Gate Park, San Francisco

Even in simple air I watch these pines,
Whose very wood has bent to the demands
Of wind, in shapes that energy defines
And keeps. But now, among the
    crouching stands

Of pine, air is becoming complicated;
The ocean fog is tumbling massively
Like spirits through the trees—like night created
Suddenly, moist with darkness, from the sea.

This is the Way: I watch yet stay within
The landscape, which is moving, cool, Chinese,
And redolent of where I've always been.
It will suffice, this life of fog and trees.

Late Afternoon Tea

This tea, neither too weak, nor strong with leaves
To etch my teeth, nor hot like licking thorns,
Recalls the attentive calm that one achieves
When purged of such desires as Plato scorns.

Chaste, it preserves an elemental poise,
Skirting extremes of water, earth, and fire
As music moves between silence and noise.
I drink. My dissonant thoughts become a choir.

Wood

Wood of the morning is a twig in spring
Aggrandized with a lucent blob of rain;
Wood of the noon is wharf-wood—
    splinter-bundles
As warm as old grey velvet; wood that's lain,

Settling, in piles for many a fall, to season,
Is of the dusk; and if you care to know
Wood of the night, walk in a redwood forest
Where in the damp the fallen laurels grow.

Structures

This is the structure of the early dawn:
Before its colors are defined like tone
In a becoming poem, there's a rest,
As when a line ends with a comma—stressed,
Slightly, but showing that the sense runs on,
That more is coming than one could have known.

*Looking across the Bay
from Berkeley to San Francisco*

While I had turned away
To watch the ever finer
Connotations of day
Behind a mountain-top,
The city had lit up;
It rode in brilliant state—
A night-bound ocean liner
Poised at the Golden Gate.

Skipping Stones on a Lake

> The penny-slim
> stone that spins
> from his arched in-
> dex finger skips
> lightly in lit-
> tle bumps, dip-
> ping elastically
> as far as we
> think we can see—
> then comes to rest,
> sinking at last.

Early Morning Spiderwebs

Thick mist, which hides the very hills
In vapid whitishness, distills
Its lucid droplets, to reveal,
In outlines that the half-light fills,
Designs that clear day will conceal.

Cyclic

The value of those time-of-year details—
Coffee-steam on cooler mornings, the smell
Of coming snow, the touch of hot wood rails—
Rose from their power suddenly to swell
The moment to a vision, to suggest
A perfect season where my thoughts could rest,
Its essence these details on which I dwell.

Fall Is for Long Journeys by Sea

Fall is for long journeys by sea,
To Europe and the festive past.
Not summer: heat and glare contrast
Too dully and obtrusively

With subtle, cool medieval tones.
October light, waning but clear,
Allows old values to appear
In church-glass, yellowed cloister-stones,

Or tapestries of love and war.
Crossing by sea is rough and slow,
Rightly: to leave the world we know
For one that promises yet more,

We need the rites of passage. Fall,
Ripe time of change, fosters them all.

Excursion behind an Old Manor-House

for Kathryn, age two

I notice how the still grey trees contrast
With flittering snow, and though you see this too,
You cannot see that what we're going through
Is like an entrance into England's past,
Veiled by the snow-like years to memory's view;

For you don't recognize the rich domain
Of history, though it's here from Tudor times,
This share of nature's realm that man designs:
The park, with its stone manor-house as plain
As snow-filled woods or Wyatt's chiselled lines.

We wandered in the snowy afternoon
Enclosed by England, by the inward mood
Of winter, deep as silence, that subdued
Our words and footfall. We'd be turning soon,
Homeward, but not from cold or solitude.

Wytham Abbey

From the perspective of a Tudor gable,
    The air is old and thin.
For as I look on gate, church, barn, and stable,
    Distance enters in;
    Time becomes clear as air;
I see the Wytham that was there.

Easy Passage

Everyday spices—cinnamon, vanilla,
Chocolate—are from the islands of the east,
All redolent of luxuries and sweets.
And thinking names like Singapore, Manila,
Java, makes fragrance echo in the mind,
With overtones of Conrad. So I find
At breakfast or dessert the scent of distance,
Of sandalwood and sails, breath of typhoons,
The clack of palmleaves, densest afternoon.
I travel as I wish, without resistance.

The Elves and the Shoemaker, Christmas Eve

Now the astonished elves behold
The finished shoes, the piece-work gone,
And pies, to warm them from the cold;
The old couple, unseen, look on.

This tale has simple sense to bestow—
A sense of gifts, feasting, and leather,
Of house and hearth, midnight and snow,
Of age and childhood glad together.

Walking in Country Lanes, Taizé, Burgundy

This is a world come down from elder times,
    Where blackbirds, geese, a crooked stile,
A market cross—known from nursery rhymes—
    Appear, to fill each crooked mile
With images half imagined, odd details
Come true, now, like wishes in fairy tales.

Village in Winter, with Skaters

The sundriness of twigs, fences, and cries
Is muted and composed by ice and snow,
Which, in their blank integrity, comprise
All wayward parts, making them darkly show.

The disarray is either edged in white—
Like bushes, branches, reeds, and window-sills—
Or smoothed, like yards and roofs.
      Blackbirds alight
Against the snow, whose cold decorum spills

Onto the ice-decked brook; there children, men,
And women, loud and fat as blackbirds, lurch
And skid, happily, resting now and then.
The ice blends with the sky and the little church.

That is their wholeness: being here, alive,
One country day in fifteen sixty-five.

Spaghetti Dinner

My brain, sublimed with wine,
Proves gluttony a sin
By choosing to resign
Its birthright, consciousness,
To my boorish stomach, which,
Stuffed like a sausage skin,
Is heedless of the switch;
Just as if Prospero,
While drunk, had tried to press
His books on Trinculo.

A Cure for Statesmen

Too old and weak to do it with your hands,
You fight with peace-talk, policies, commands.
You suffer from abstraction. Here's a cure,
To make the game concrete, less falsely pure:
Each time a body's torn or scorched, a pin
Should mark that spot upon a map—your skin.
And though your name were legion, you'd get
    your due;
There'd be enough to cover all of you.

Memorandum for Mr. Reagan, from the Academy
Berkeley, California, 1969.

To win the populace
You spurn the academy,
So hoping to impress
Yourself on history.

We offer a humble threat:
Temper this heat that brooks
No light, lest you forget
Who writes the history-books.

Cat

She is a wreath of smoke, but thick.
Now she awakens. See each thought
Move as she moves, fluent and quick,
Like words that spring to the tongue unsought.

Moments contain her, one by one.
She thinks as far as she can see;
Yet she will break a food-bent run
To plunge, savagely, for a flea.

Such limits free her. Though more clever,
We do not live as if forever.

A Free Moment

Reticulated cracks
In pale
Green shale
Draw my attention;
Exquisite things attract
Firm thought.
When taut—
Trembling with tension—
My mind does not react
To pale
Green shale.

Reduction

When I subtract
All memories, facts,
Intelligence,
The body-senses,
Pleasure, pain—
Everything
I feel or think—
Something remains;
Is it myself
Or someone else?

Consciousness

It is projected from your brain—
A sheer ribbon of light
That turns in spiral, curve, and plane
Between the halves of night.

The Roaring of the Fire

The roaring of the fire is not the fire;
It is the wind by which all flames aspire
To smoke. Such spirits likewise animate
Your life, whose consequence is ash, whose state,
Exalted now, can rise only as smoke.

Whether your substance be of straw or oak,
The wind will blow at will, the ashes wait.

Time is the Fire

Time is the fire in which we gently burn.
It cooks the fat from our tissues, crisps our skin,
And dries each bone till brittle, while we turn
On some assumed intent, wholly exposed,
Ever more deeply touched from outside in,
Till fire becomes the flesh in which we're closed.

Jesuit Graveyard, Ash Wednesday

Neither abandoned meadow, nor as neat
As a golfcourse-cemetery where defeat
Is marked by fond inscriptions, soft on hard,
Sweet sculpture for the dead—this is a yard
Behind a college, kept in decent form,
With random pine-trees counterpointing
    the norm
Of ordered stone. The graves are spaced by rows
Of crosses; at the bases dark clay shows
Against the white of marble, but higher up
Their names and years for good are cleanly cut
As if on tablets in the Book of Life.
Transfigured death is bright, not dark; no wife,
No child has mourned these men, and when
    they died
They triumphed, in a last defeat of pride.
This is their field. Foraging robins scatter
The dust, to litanies of squirrels' chatter.

The Burial of Christ: from the Sterzingen Altarpiece

Two patricians lower his head, his feet,
Both now unmindful of stately beard and gown.
With folds like sculptured marble, the winding-sheet
Conceals their hands, precedes the body down,

Fold over fold, into the oblong tomb.
But Christ, his forearms crossed, is in repose
Above that chasm, light upon its gloom.
His agony, once awesome, only shows

Through dots on hands and feet, and, on his side,
A crescent, brown as rust. His eyes seem closed
In contemplation, as though they had not died;
His features, like his hands, are thin, composed.

The women minister, their eyes downcast.
The churchyard path goes through a gate, then past
Embankments, trees, the hill that bears the Tree,
To a walled medieval town in Germany.

Scripture Lesson

Judas, one of the chosen,
For thirty pieces sold him;
Thomas's faith was pale;
Peter, when tested, failed.
Chosen people are never
Dependable. But devils,
Madmen, the sick, the blind,
Discerned him every time.

Prayer for Himself

The child I was, gone but not dead,
Lives in this dome of heaven—my head.
In retrospect I cherish him
Who at the time could never shed
Self-hatred, as one sheds a skin.
May He that keeps what is alive,
And leaves as cast-off flesh our sin,
Cherish me thus when I arrive.

The Last Judgment

Medieval sculptors knew,
Better than marxists, what to do
With the exploiting upper classes:
You carve them naked into stone,
With fiends that strip them to the bone
While shoving skewers up their asses.
Torture them richly and with skill.
And let them pay the bill.

Fourteenth Century Fresco, St. Pierre, Brançion

It's Resurrection Day
Six hundred years ago:
Look at the little men,
Women, and children climb
From tombs as from a bath,
Naked from head to toe,
With bodies back again
And smiles to cheer God's wrath.
Surely this is the way
To greet the end of time.

To Andrei Rublev

It's snowing in your church's burnt-out skull;
Blood has frozen to stained glass in the streets;
Tartars, not monks, are at Andronikov.
But you, who neither weep nor curse nor scoff,
You understand, and paint the Trinity.
They have one face. Its mutual gaze meets
Beyond their halos, which are gold but dull,
As if to sharpen the serenity.

The Logos

So dense with being that his thoughts take flesh,
God is meaning. We are his words; we mesh
With him as intimately as word with thought.
He will recall us from oblivion,
Remembering all that history had forgot,
Putting together what he'd said and done.